Turn Left To Power

A Road Map
For Labour

By

Malcolm Blair-Robinson

Contents

Foreword

1

Reflections

2

Review of Options

3

Rebalancing the Economy

4

Restoring Democratic Links

5

Responsibility of Government

6

Reforming Taxation

7

Reconnecting Labour to Power

8

Rebooting the Nation

Afterword

By the same Author

Fiction

The Judas Cross

Downfall in Downing Street

Stanislaw's Crossing

A Gift of Treason

Hitler's First Lady

Purple Killing

Non-Fiction

2010 A Blueprint for Change

Dynamic Quantitative Easing

Writing as Tor Raven

The Hess Enigma

This first edition is published before the outcome of the EU Referendum is known. However the conclusions and recommendations would not substantially vary with either result.

Foreword

A Warning

Clinging to the false wisdom that power beckons from the trampled and muddy centre of politics is an illusion from which Labour must escape.

There is a good deal of confusion about why the Labour party lost the 2015 general election. This has not been helped by various inquiries about the disaster having a much to say, but missing the point or even promoting findings to suit the centrist view. In UK national elections, with the first past the post electoral system, victories are celebrated in seats, but defeats must be analysed in votes. Votes tell an interesting contra-intuitive story.

The Tories won the general election on the lowest winning vote the party has achieved since well before WWII. Cameron had 11.3 million votes. Churchill lost in 1950 on a smaller franchise (you had to be twenty-one to vote) with 12.5 million. In 1950 the population had just hit 50 million. So he achieved the support of 25% of the all the people in the UK and he lost for the second time. In 2015 the population was 64 million.

This gave Cameron just 17%. But he won outright with a majority for the first time.

Of course not everybody in the population has the right to vote and some do not bother even to register. If we look at the registered voters in 2015, we find there were 46.4 million. 30.6 million actually turned out. Put another way, 16 million stayed at home. Another 3.8 million voted for UKIP. The majority of those missing votes who could be persuaded to go to the polls would go to Labour, if New Labour had not abandoned their cause. New Labour, which is near extinct in the country, but dominates the parliamentary Labour party, is in denial about what is happening. Here are the figures.

In 1992 Kinnock lost with 11.5 million votes. In 1997 Blair won with 13.5 million. This was the moment of hope at the end of Thatcherism, when New Labour was going to make a difference. But did it? In certain ways it did. The Human Rights Act was incorporated into British law, devolution was given to Scotland and Wales, the Good Friday agreement brought about peace in Northern Ireland and further strides were made against discrimination of all kinds. But the Thatcher market driven economic settlement remained not only in place but extended, creating greater gaps between rich and poor and extraordinary economic distortions. Some people did very well and many very well indeed, but they were not traditional Labour supporters.

New Labour was perhaps Thatcher's greatest political achievement and when the next election came in 2001, 2.8 million disillusioned Labour voters walked away and stayed at home. Blair still won but turnout crashed from over 70% to 59%. The working class, having discovered that their champion was fully engaged in cosying up to the City and unwilling to reverse Thatcher's excesses, felt abandoned. In 2005 another 1.2 million walked off, but Blair still won because of Tory weaknesses. Finally in 2010 there was a further drop of a shade under a million. In 2015 for the first time in seventeen years, during which it tallied a loss of 5 million votes, Labour's vote actually went up.

The figures are very much more interesting than at first they appear. In 2010 Labour dived to votes of a mere 8.6 million. But in 2015 the total rose to 9.3 million. This was the first election that the New in Labour was missing. Unfortunately so was a proper narrative and a convincing message about the economy. Nevertheless a slight move to the left not only stopped the decline in support, but did so better than even Labour realised. This is where we bring in Scotland.

The left leaning SNP wiped Labour out in Scotland, polling an extra 960 thousand votes, most coming from Labour. If we cautiously take the Labour loss at 700 thousand in Scotland, that brings the net gain in England and Wales up to 1.4 million votes, twice as many as that achieved by the Tories and a remarkable reversal of the continuous haemorrhage of support of the New Labour era. Those who assert that Labour needs to remain a centre party are way off the mark. Labour can only win from the left.

There are three elements to this. The first is that the Tory party has shifted centre left, leaving no room for another party in the same space. The second is the whole country, especially the young, senses that things are not right or fair or working and that big change is called for. The centre cannot by definition be the agent of fundamental change. The third is that victory will come not from Tory desertions to Labour but from Labour pulling out its core supporters from the millions of non-voters and from the 4 million who voted UKIP, two thirds of whom should have voted Labour.

The added challenge is this will have to be done in England and Wales. Because of uncertainties over the UK and the EU, there is new uncertainty about Scotland and the UK. In any event the SNP has not just defeated Labour north of the border, because it was perceived too close to the Tories; it has replaced it. For Labour to recover its losses in Scotland in 2020, it will require either a spectacular shipwreck for the SNP or a UK landslide for Labour. The second is actually more likely than the first.

It will not be possible to achieve a landslide, or even scrape a narrow victory, with some soft centre tinkering which merely changes the tone of the status quo. The surge in membership of the Labour party, following its election of a left wing leader, confirms the electoral potential.

What is needed to bring the vast disillusioned cohort back into the democratic process, is a fundamental change to the economic settlement, the structure of governance and the political management of the state, no less radical than Attlee's programme in 1945 or Margaret Thatcher's attack on the State which began in earnest after her victory in 1983.

Millions of ordinary people, for whose interests the Labour movement was founded to champion and upon whom the functioning of a civilised nation depends, will be hoping Labour does not let them down again. It will not survive if it does. The lessons of the millions of absent votes, the millions who voted UKIP and the wipe out in Scotland reinforces this.

This dissertation is not a detailed plan, but a brief outline of a set of fundamental reforms which would change the political weather. These reforms would secure the foundation of a radically different economic and political model which would indeed work for the many, not just the few. It is best thought of as a road map. The logistics of the journey are for Labour to plan.

1

Reflections

If you are young and in a hurry you may not want to bother with this first part, because it is more about me than it is about new ideas to set our country on a better path. You can go straight to Part 2 and either ignore this altogether or return later. The important thing is the Road Map, not its author. Because it will be your journey into the future.

For readers who are interested, this opening section offers some of the reasons why I have decided to write this. I have led a rather unscripted life. I was born in 1939 when Neville Chamberlin was Prime Minister, Franklin Roosevelt was still in his second term, Adolf Hitler was Chancellor of Germany, and Stalin ruled Russia. I was a child during World War Two and became a teenager before food rationing ended.

When peace came at last, I remember adults constantly used '*before the war*' as a nostalgic phrase of comparison. I was aware that in this nostalgic period goods and food had been plentiful and cheap. But not everything had been better. While we were now in the cold grip of rationing, shortages and make do, which people called austerity, there was a sense that much had been wrong and unfair in the pre-war past. A big national effort was in hand to make life better for everyone, and not just those who had better jobs or were better off.

Something called the Welfare State was being ushered in by the new Labour government, led by Clement Attlee (1945-51). He had been deputy prime minister throughout Churchill's period as wartime leader, so he was very experienced when he took over after the landslide win of 1945. Welfare State was not then a term of derision but of pride, except among a few reactionaries who had no need of its help. The state was seen not as an obstacle or a hindrance but as an essential framework for civilisation which would protect everyone at all times and, when you were in need, could provide. The state was not an enemy, ogre or something to mistrust and fear; it was the fabric of the nation, for which two great wars had been fought to protect and to preserve. The wars had shown how the state could be used to mobilise the nation to give of its united best.

The state was being used in peacetime to lift the standard of living and quality of life for everyone through full employment, free healthcare and education, slum clearance, massive affordable house building and world leading innovation. It owned and ran the coal mines, railways and most bus services, all the public utilities and the steel industry. So in spite of the shortages, the threadbare clothes and the old fashioned cars from years gone by but kept running, there was a sense of optimism that times were all the while getting better and the bad old days, when the few had more than half of everything, were sliding into the past.

Today I find myself living in a very different country. The rich are getting richer but the gap between rich and poor is growing. Once again the few have more than half of everything. The old balance between capital and labour, sustained by a necessary tension between the two acting as a brake on excess by either, has gone. The power of capital is now unchallenged and the instrument of its power, lending, is the driver of everything. It used not to be like this. And it does not have to be. There is another way forward.

When I was eighteen I joined the Young Conservatives. Harold Macmillan was Prime Minister (1957-1962). The YCs, as they were universally known, were the largest political youth organisation in the free world. The Tory party was, and saw itself as, a moderate party of one nation tradition. It was well to the left of what became New Labour. When I grew older I remained an enthusiastic supporter and even toyed with a career in politics. I was at one time nearly the youngest on the list of approved prospective parliamentary candidates at Conservative Central Office.

In 1963 Macmillan became ill with what he mistakenly thought was prostate cancer and supposed himself to be dying, so he resigned as prime minister in a chaotic chain of events. The Conservative Party Conference was in full swing when news of his illness and transfer to hospital broke and contenders to replace him began an unseemly process to garner support. Meanwhile in London the Queen visited her prime minister in his hospital room to receive his resignation from his bed, probably an historic first. In those days it was the custom that the retiring PM should nominate his successor, there was no democracy in the Tory party at this level; the theory was that the leader 'emerged'.

There were various potential candidates emerging at the conference which had become a cauldron of plotting and rumour. The strongest was R.A.Butler, Macmillan's deputy, and had there been an election he would most likely have won. But Macmillan was determined he should not get the prize and a flabbergasted nation learned the Queen had sent for the foreign secretary, the Earl of Home, who as Lord Dunglass, his title before he inherited, had been Chamberlain's bag carrier at Munich, when the former signed the infamous 'peace in our time' agreement with Hitler in 1938.

Home was Macmillan's popular and effective foreign secretary but he sat in the House of Lords through inheritance, rather than in the House of Commons through election. An inherited prime minister leading from the Lords was a preposterous notion even in those days, but there was a magic twist to the tale. Tony Benn, who was not quite so left as he later became and was known as Antony Wedgewood-Benn, had rebelled against being forced by law to inherit his father's title, Viscount Stansgate, and legislation had been enacted to enable for a short period peers to renounce their titles and seek election to the Commons. Benn took advantage of this as so did Home, who became prime minister until the general election in 1964, when he lost to Harold Wilson. In fact Sir Alec Douglas-Home, as he became known, was quite a good leader and did very much better than everyone expected.

In the run up to the general election of 1964 Sir Alec undertook a whistle stop tour of Kent, my home county, marginal constituencies. I heard about this at the planning stage and bold opportunist as I then was, offered my services on the day with my car, something that not everyone had in those days. I found myself attached to the prime ministerial motorcade which I picked up at Bexley (Heath's constituency) with the duty of setting off about five minutes before the end of the PM's speech at one venue so as to warn of his pending arrival at the next. This was well before the smartphone era.

All went well to start with, but as the morning wore on and traffic built up I kept seeing the PM coming up in my mirror, because he had a police escort to clear the traffic. So it was decided mid-morning that I too should have an escort, my own police motor cycles, fore and aft. I cannot describe to you the thrill of charging through traffic at up to sixty miles an hour on the wrong side of the road, over red lights, traffic parting before my eyes, like Moses parting the waves. Or to put it in modern terms, it was definitely a Clarkson moment.

The tour ended in the marginal seat of Dover in time for afternoon tea and an hour later Sir Alec boarded a flimsy light aircraft and flew to Balmoral to ask the Queen for a Dissolution of Parliament, so that the election could campaign could begin in earnest. After the Tory defeat and the arrival of the first Wilson premiership for Labour (1964-70) I applied to join the official list of Conservative prospective parliamentary candidates and was surprised to be accepted without much trouble.

After being short listed for one constituency but unsuccessful at the final hurdle, the responsibility of a young family drove me towards earning a reliable living and away from political engagement. Shortly after Heath became Prime Minister (1970-74) I found myself in the City as a director of an insurance company. Doubts about the direction of travel of my favoured political party began to set in as a new generation of rather inexperienced Tory grandees caused the government to swing from consensus to confusion and in the two elections which Heath fought in 1974 I voted Liberal. Looking back I think I began to see, for the first time in my life, what you might call the other side of the coin.

My middle class upbringing and private education, with an invalid father and the modest family income derived from a trust fund, gave me an establishment view of everything. Working in London I mixed with a wider social spectrum and saw that not everything was as it had seemed. Moreover I learned also that not everything about business was good. I think that politically I remained on the right, whilst drifting slowly to the left over the next forty years. I did not arrive with conviction until detailed research post the 2008 crash finally convinced me that our current economic model is not only unfair and undesirable but also unsustainable. So in 2015 I voted Labour for the first time. But a lot happened first.

The 1970s were torrid politically for both the main parties. The sudden doubling of the oil price by the Arab producers, upon whose production the UK was almost entirely dependent, caused an instant financial crisis. Heath's government first U turned over economic policy then lost control of events and faced wild inflation, a miner's strike, power cuts and a three day working week because of lack of electricity, which eventually brought down the government. Inflation was out of control and the miners were demanding a wage increase of 37.5%. Early in 1974 Heath called a general election on the theme, who governs Britain?

Not you! Said the electorate. Heath lost, but only just. Labour had more seats but no majority. Heath tried to persuade the Liberals to join him to form a majority government, but their leader Jeremy Thorpe, put it to his MPs and they voted No. Perhaps they saw power as a poisoned chalice.

Harold Wilson, who had remained leader of the Labour party after its defeat in 1970, it was not then expected for party leaders to throw in the towel the moment they lost, formed a minority Labour government, for which he gained a wafer thin majority at a second election in the autumn of the same year. He then resigned as prime minister in 1976 for no apparent reason, giving his age as the driver of his decision.

His replacement, Jim Callaghan, was actually older. Sadly Wilson knew by then he was in the early stages of Alzheimer's, so he acted bravely in the interests of the country. He was good at winning elections, and won four, but although popular with Labour voters, never appealed across party lines as a national leader. Callaghan did appeal more widely, but lost the only general election he fought as prime minister.

His government had seen its slim majority wither and disappear through by-election losses. Labour had been unable to bring order to the mess left by Heath and had to call in the IMF for a bailout because the public finances were all but bust. This involved national humiliation of an especially wounding kind for the former Empire, now dubbed by the Americans as the Sick Man of Europe. A team of IMF officials set up residence in Brown's Hotel in London and began a review of the nation's accounts. They then wrote a letter laying out terms and conditions which would have to be met to get some cash. The government was obliged to agree. It was not a good moment.

Callaghan gave power to the unions which they seriously misused. Inflation, which had spun out of control under Heath, could not be suppressed although it fell back from its 1974 peak of 25% per annum. To survive, Callaghan fixed a deal with the Liberals known as the Lib Lab pact. This did not involve the Liberals joining the government but it did ensure its survival in exchange for some Liberal input on policy decisions.

Eventually the pact collapsed and Callaghan was defeated on a vote of confidence proposed by the new Tory leader Margaret Thatcher. The government fell. The Iron Lady, as the Soviets had christened her because she said nasty things about them, won the resulting general election comfortably and became our first and so far only woman prime minister (1979-1990). The catalyst for this change of power, which heralded a shift of the centre to the right, was the 1978/79 Winter of Discontent.

This was period of so much industrial unrest that millions of working days were being lost for little to no reason over contrived disputes. The climax came when the public sector unions stopped the collection of rubbish so that it was piled high in the streets and in a giant mountain in London's Leicester Square, which was commandeered as an emergency tip for public use. Finally the grave diggers stopped working and the dead lay unburied in refrigeration plants with funerals halted. The public had had enough. In came Thatcher with her monetarist nostrums, which signalled the gradual unravelling of the whole post war consensus. Labour was denied another go in four consecutive general elections.

I did not take to Margaret Thatcher and never voted for her. She was too far to the right for me, too socially divisive and too simplistic in many of her solutions. But she was a great Prime Minister in the full sense of the word and changed her country out of all recognition. She inaugurated a revival of national pride and purpose. She moved the centre ground of politics far to the right and created a new consensus which demonized the welfare state as the loser's option and destroyed the notion that personal gain must at the same time enhance the public good.

She bludgeoned the unions into submission and brought order to industrial relations, but with various financial reforms and deregulations, she set in train forces in the City which ran out of control. She believed in market forces as the primary economic engine that would always find their own level which would be the right one. Regulation simply hindered their smooth working and should be cut back. She saw no role for the state in business or public utilities and sold off almost everything the government owned except the armed forces. The word privatisation was coined to explain this process.

She inaugurated a housing shortage from which we still suffer by selling off council houses and taking the money straight to the exchequer so that councils could not replace their depleting stocks. Having won three general elections in a row she went on an ego trip, declaring that she would go on and on. She ignored every informed piece of advice that disaster beckoned and drove through the Poll Tax. The resulting riots across the country were an unprecedented response to a government policy. Her cabinet recoiled. They stabbed her in the back and she was gone. The Thatcher era was over but Thatcherism lived on to be inherited, dressed in pink to make it softer, by New Labour.

Labour reacted to her initial election victory by failing to see that the centre had moved to the right. It chose the ultra-left idealist Michael Foot as leader. This proved a disaster not only with the electors, but also for the party which began to break up. Left wing activists held de-selection meetings to get rid of moderate MPs and extremist regimes ruled in Labour's name in Liverpool and Southwark. An organisation called the Militant Tendency went on the rampage through the party. The function of the official opposition became fragmented and disorganised. My leftward drift stalled at this spectacle. I felt there surely must be a voice of reason somewhere left of centre, but short of the Marxist mayhem now unfolding.

Eventually four of Labour's most senior moderates, Roy Jenkins, David Owen, Shirley Williams and Bill Rodgers, went into open rebellion and in January 1981 met to conspire together in Owens's house in Docklands. They emerged to unveil something they called The Limehouse Declaration. This inaugurated an organisation called The Council for Social Democracy. It was all about Social Democracy in the European style of the centre left and was to be caring and pragmatic rather than radical and challenging.

This very much appealed to me and I joined on the first day. I then migrated across when a few weeks later it transformed itself into the Social Democratic Party, known as the SDP. Because I was a former Conservative, I was welcomed into the new party with a personal meeting with Roy Jenkins at his pad in Notting Hill. Later I took a carload of members including, my wife and my eldest son, up to Warrington to canvass for him in the famous by-election. I had one or two further meetings with Jenkins at the House of Commons when he finally won a Scottish seat. He was engaging and entertaining, very cerebral, but I always felt more of an idealist than a cunning politician. He became a brilliant political biographer.

I saw the SDP not so much as a new party of the left but a potential successor to the one nation Conservatism of the Macmillan era. I became the Chairman of the City of London and Westminster South constituency and later the same role at Folkestone and Hythe in the election of 1983, when Michal Howard won the constituency, a safe Tory seat, and entered parliament for the first time. Our man, under the seat sharing agreement known as the Alliance, was a Liberal and a well-known QC like his opponent. He was convinced he had won right up to the count, when he lost big.

I could see little point in the amalgamation with the Liberals and stayed with David Owen, who refused to join his colleagues and reconstituted the SDP under his own leadership. I remember chairing a very well attended public meeting in Canterbury at which he was the star. He could certainly pull a crowd on a rainy night. Meanwhile Neil Kinnock had become Labour leader and had begun the reconstruction of the party into a united an effective opposition, which was left wing but not loony left. He had to fight many battles with activists but succeeded in pulling the Labour party back from the brink.

There was no room for three parties of the left and the SDP was the smallest. It still had a core of devotees but its élan was faded and its future uncertain. When it sank in 1990 after collapsing as a political force, I went down with the ship. I have not been politically active since. In many ways Blair became the alternative with New Labour, but he was little more than a pink Thatcherite to me, with dangerous judgement shortfalls, as we discovered. But he was a winner, and sadly in modern politics winning is everything.

Life changing events are rarely foreseen. In my case a second marriage and two more children (making a total of six) created a chain of events which were outside my experience, engaged my worst fears, challenged my most sensitive inhibitions and opened up a whole new understanding of life. Our youngest child, a delightful little girl who charmed all who came into contact with her, was born with a congenital condition to which she finally succumbed. At the age of twelve she died in our arms. Nothing can prepare you for that, nor can you imagine the pain which follows.

Her mother, her sister and I will carry that moment with us always, but we have learned how to accept it as a strength which can guide us onward and enrich our lives. It taught me how to think. Or more particularly to analyse complex problems for which there were no obvious answers which worked, reduce the issue to the basics and then find a way forward. When it is the life of a loved one that hangs by a thread, you learn fast.

In the year following our daughter's death, the global financial system collapsed in 2008. As the drama of the UK banks going down happened while I was in bed with bronchitis, I watched the whole thing evolve on rolling news. I had for years been saying that it was impossible for asset values, especially property, to continuously inflate through ever higher borrowing on lax financial diligence without something snapping, but I had imagined that I was just making conversation without the qualifications to say anything which might come true. Experts would know how to manage the risks. Not only did it turn out that they did not, but worse, many had not even seen the risks.

I began to carry out my own research and to apply a good deal of thinking to the outcome. It was apparent that economics was not a science but a discipline, in which there were as many threads and opinions as there were stars in the sky. So it was necessary to dig even deeper to get right down to the fundamentals, and then build solutions which were sanitized against infection from economic dogma and discord. This is not to say that all economists are wrong; it acknowledges that there are varying interpretations and competing theories about almost everything and the nature of the issues makes outcomes hard to predict. It also became clear that an approach which worked in one era could fail when applied to another.

Most economists have a particular 'line' which they favour, and politicians tend attach themselves to one of these. This is the key. Much of it is intrinsically bound up with political theory and dependent on human behaviour. A theory can be mathematically neat but socially unworkable. I became interested in the process of Quantitative Easing, which is a modern way of printing money electronically to inject new cash into an economy seizing up through lack of liquidity. It was used by both the Federal Reserve in Washington and the Bank of England in London to kick start the American and British economies after the crash. These two economies became the fastest growing of the industrialised nations. The problem with the process is that it boosts the financial sector, already too big in the UK, whilst taking a long time to trickle down to the real economy and then only as lending which has to be repaid.

I researched previous times of economic stress and as far as I could discover printing money through Treasury bank notes had helped to finance WWI and something called Treasury Direct Deposits had been sparingly used in the aftermath of WWII. I devised a new version which I called Dynamic Quantitative Easing, which was designed to fuel economic growth from the base, rather than the top, of the economy by bypassing the financial structure altogether. I described this idea in a paper which I sent to the then governor of the Bank of England, Mervyn King. Within a few days I was excited to receive a warm and generous personal reply from him encouraging me to put my ideas forward.

I was so astonished that I did nothing for a further two years. This was partly because I was rather busy writing novels, particularly those involving hidden political secrets of World War Two, which required a good deal of concentration. Eventually I decided to publish the paper through Amazon's platforms both in e-book and paperback, but to publicize it only on my own current affairs blog, without any public relations trail. To make it a little more entertaining I added a section of blog posts from the early part of 2015. One or two copies were mailed here and there, including to the TUC. There was interest there and I was invited to meet the chief economist.

It was clear that whilst the Tories were confident with their economic policy, the left as defined by the Labour movement, was less clear cut in its position; a bit more of this and less of that, but surely not enough of anything to win. I explained that I was not after personal power or fame. But I did want to put a useful tool into the hands of those who could put it to good use. I came away with a feeling that in economic terms my proposal might be a new idea in town.

I am not an economist and do not pretend to be. But I have a lifetime of experience as a political observer and fringe participant; I have a regular current affairs blog which specializes in international affairs, economics and politics which contains not far short of a million words. On politics and strategic economics I am an innovative thinker. After the general election returned an unexpected Tory majority, narrow overall but big in England, I realised that it may not be enough to have floated an economic theory on its own.

To give it form and thus give it force, it would have to be put into a political context. To do that I began to re-examine the political realities of this country in a way I had not done for decades, if ever. I had already asked myself basic questions like what capitalism is and what money is. Now I asked, what is democracy? And what are the ingredients which make it work well? The rest of this book explains the results of this process in a way which I hope you will find easy to follow.

If you do, I hope it will fire up your imagination so that you can see ways forward for you and your family which had not occurred to you before. It should help to clarify notions of personal value and national purpose which have become confused in recent years and somewhat self-centred. It may even inspire you to step forward and do something to help your country. That would be really good.

For it is now the case that by misunderstandings and good intentions which fell short, we have created a society in which *the rich grow richer at the expense of the poor*. How and why this has happened, how it can be corrected and who should be the instrument of change, are the messages this thin volume is intended to convey. On a more positive note we have succeeded in building a society which is free under the law of discrimination on grounds of sex, sexual orientation, age, race and religion. This is a huge achievement. We now need an economic model to match it. We will then release the full potential of all the people. There is no such thing as a loser. But far too few are winners. Together we can change that.

I end this explanation with a golden political rule. Governments come and go and most people hardly notice. But every so often a winning combination occurs which brings about change and renewal which informs the consensus thereafter for at least a generation. It happened with Attlee in 1945 and Thatcher in 1979. It is when a fresh economic theory, the public mood, the desire for social renewal and political leadership fall into harmony either on the left or the right. They create a winning combination which changes perceptions. And they come from opposite ends of the political spectrum, because they arise out of the excesses of the last revision.

Attlee took the nation far to the left. Thatcher shifted it to the right. It is time to move left again, but down a very different road to before. Both those political giants carried a fresh approach to economics which became embedded. If the left is now

to have a revival which endures, it will have to come forward with bold new ideas for a national revival and a fairer economic settlement which builds lasting growth to bring prosperity for the many as well as the few.

2

Review of Options

We can summarise the predicament of the UK as one in which an economy once powered by coal and manufacturing has become one powered by debt and consumption. Debt brings profit to capital but sucks savings from labour. Because of the high value of the currency, imports are cheaper than home produced goods, causing too much of the benefits of consumption to flow out of the country, leaving the base of the economy unable to generate new wealth.

The knock on effects have produced a widening of the gap between rich and poor, a lack of skills in the workforce matched by a lack of jobs for young people with higher education achievement. The UK has the largest external debt mountain of any country in the world except the US and the lowest productivity of any of the industrialised nations. Working hours are the longest in Europe. Family life is significantly under strain and too many cases has broken down altogether.

This is a process which has developed over the thirty five years of what can be called the

Thatcher consensus and is as much the responsibility of New Labour as of the Tories. In fact New Labour is the more culpable because it engaged for the sake of power, a hedonistic culture which the Labour Movement was founded to challenge and had always previously opposed. The Tories have never pretended to be other than the party of the establishment and capital, with power as their natural expectation, so they cannot be blamed for looking after their interests.

But Labour's job is to look after the interests of the many, not as a glossy spin of good intentions but as a fact of policy and governance. Blair won his first election promising to make a difference, which was achieved at the margin but not for the whole. There were high points, but not many.

Sadly the negatives are everywhere felt by a multitude betrayed by an Oxbridge political elite out of its depth, which stood by smugly hobnobbing with what it called the filthy rich, whilst an economic monster was assembled before its eyes. The well-off have never had it better, but below those few there are unprecedented levels of inequality, social dysfunction and economic hardship. A revitalised Labour Movement must abandon its addiction to power without clear purpose and return to its roots among the ordinary people of our country, who wait in bewilderment at the impotence of their former champion. Taking up the cause of the many, upon whom the workings of a fair, prosperous and civilised society depend, will restore the purpose and deliver the power.

Here are two key reforms which, when delivered, will herald a complete change.

An innovative economic policy which abandons austerity to grow and rebalance the economy without borrowing. It will shift dominance away from the City and back to the shop floor, workshop, construction site and infrastructure project as well as revitalizing the culture of neighbourhood SMEs. It will create enough new wealth to expand the economy, through manufacturing for home consumption and for exports and infrastructure renewal, and to pay for fully funded healthcare, education, social care and other benefits and public services. It will include up to two million new homes owned by local authorities or housing associations, to provide long term security to tenants at realistic rents, free of the need for the housing benefit subsidy of private sector landlords.

A restoration of democratic accountability for what has become a shadow state administered by quangos, paid for by taxpayers, composed of privately owned agencies and contractors carrying out monopoly functions independent of Government. The rule should be if taxpayers foot the bills, the organisation is publicly owned, part of the appropriate ministry or local authority and the responsibility of the minister or council. The State has been made apparently smaller but the slack has been taken up by a new private sector which is funded by the state, often for the profit of shareholders, held in check by a network of regulators armed with millions of regulations. This cumbersome, complex and unwieldy agglomeration consumes public money, yet its line of democratic accountability is so diffuse as to be beyond the reach of the people who pay its bills.

Fix these two key areas of stress and a rejuvenation of British Values within all public policy will follow. That will deliver a fairer society which shares both burdens and rewards more equally, in which the state plays a positive role in the advance of better times, while enabling the private sector to play its part to the full. Innovation and aspiration should be championed within a golden rule that in the end everything is for the public good.

Once again we must recognise the role of the vast majority of working people at all levels, whose pay is naturally subject to limitations otherwise costs become unsustainable. Their contribution is fundamental to the working of a civilised nation. A society which considers it right to pay a chief executive of a top company an average of £4.5 million a year to serve the interests of shareholders, while at the same time paying a nurse in a top hospital an average of £25,000 to save the lives of the sick, has not only lost the moral integrity of its values. It has lost its pride in its purpose and the nobility of its endeavour.

3

Rebalancing the Economy

We must now take time to look at the economic specifics, because it is a lack of specifics which have caused Labour's failure to articulate a credible alternative to austerity. (*If economic detail leaves you seriously cold move on to* **4**). Not only is the current economic model deeply flawed and unfair, it is dangerously dependent on global events outside its control. No economy in the modern world can be insulated, but increasing turbulence in world markets and uncertainties about where the Chinese economy is headed, indicate testing times are approaching.

Economics is not a finite discipline. It has all sorts of elements and these perform in different ways in different circumstances. Economists and politicians differ in their interpretation of the variability and impact of different options and often become associated with a particular combination. What works in one set of circumstances will fail in another. Whoever gains will cause others to lose. Whatever the choice, if used carefully, it will yield a positive outcome if applied to a situation which requires it, but if used to excess it will makes matters worse. Like medicine or ingredients in cooking, the measure is critical. What follows is my recipe for Labour to adopt for the times in which we are living now. It is bold and different and looks to the future, whilst remembering the past.

At first an economy driven by home consumption looks more secure, but when you factor in that it is fed by imports financed by borrowing and its product is being used to fund excessive house price inflation, things look a lot darker. Labour has to have strong answers and ambitious plans to effect real change. It cannot offer an economic face lift. It has to come forward with a much more attractive model.

When the banks and City institutions ran out of money, the government at first borrowed, but when the scale of the problem became clear, it allowed the Bank of England to print money, known as *Quantitative Easing*. The Americans did the same. The numbers are eye watering. The Bank of England (BoE) printed £375 billion and the Federal Reserve Bank (the Fed) printed over $4 trillion. The method used by the Fed was to purchase government bonds and mortgage securities with new money created electronically. The BoE restricted its purchases to mainly government bonds. The exercise has been very successful and stabilized a financial system on the brink of collapse. It is the prime reason why both the US and UK economies have been the fastest growing in the post-crash era.

The problem with QE is that it tends to inflate assets without creating new wealth. As with any form of QE, inflation is a risk. In the case of the UK QE, inflation has been well managed, but assets, especially property and shares, rose in value much faster than inflation overall and very much faster than earnings at the base of the economy. That increases inequality, reduces the tax base and increases welfare spending. QE favours capital over labour and while it restored the financial sector it has left the real economy trailing far behind.

To rebalance the economy to give labour a better deal, I advocate a variation of QE which I call *Dynamic Quantitative Easing*. The difference is that while QE is printed by the central bank within its remit of independent responsibility for financial management, in our case the Bank of

England, DQE is printed by the Treasury, but to do it is a political decision within the democratic responsibility for economic management. It remains under the control of the elected government.

Instead of entering the banking system to shore up balance sheets or to pass on for personal and business lending like QE, DQE goes straight into the government's bank accounts as cash, to be used for investment in infrastructure renewal, social house building and grants for start-up businesses. There is no borrowing anywhere in the chain. DQE puts real money into circulation at the base of the economy to balance the debt driven overhang at the top.

DQE has to be carefully managed to avoid triggering excessive inflation. The danger comes from an excess of money and scarcity of skilled labour or a shortage of raw materials driving up costs which are then passed on. It would therefore follow that the new money would have to be introduced in stages. Theoretically it should be sufficient to introduce the same amount as QE, £375 billion, over the course of a parliament. This would amount to an exceptional stimulus of the working economy.

The object is to secure growth which starts at the base and rises upwards. Overall the UK economy needs to achieve 5% growth *at least,* each year for several years in order to expand its tax base sufficiently to pay for all the public services for which there is a real need, without wasting tens of billions each year subsidising out of control rents or earnings which are too low to meet the cost of living.

Additionally it is important to consider the balance of trade; this is the difference between what we import and what we export. For many years the United Kingdom has run a deficit. At one time this used to be a hot political issue, but nowadays it is hardly mentioned. In cash terms we import about £100 billion worth of goods each year more than we export. In GDP terms the latest figure is expressed as 5.5%. This is the highest of any of the industrialised countries. That is serious not just because we are not paying our way, but also because it means that we are exporting both the jobs and skills that home manufacture and production would normally provide. DQE would exert downward pressure on sterling, which would help to make British goods more competitive. It would also make imports more expensive, creating a better climate for a reboot of home production of more of the things we consume.

As we have seen, the epicentre of our difficulties lies an excess of debt and a shortage of money. Politicians shrink from the notion of printing money, sighting the Zimbabwe or post WW1 Germany currency collapses as reasons why not.

The problem is that to re-boot a stagnant economy without money is the same as trying to cook without heat. It will not happen. So the fashion has been to borrow. The trouble with borrowing is that it results in debt. Debt costs. It sucks money back in interest payments, it has to be repaid and if not restrained becomes both too big to service and too big to repay. We no longer dig money from the ground in the form of coal and our oil production is falling. The American recovery is much broader based than that of the UK because of its strength in manufacturing and the high tech industries and also because the drive for fracking has transformed it from an energy importing economy to one nearing self-sufficiency, giving the important advantage of a steady flow of new wealth into the base of the economy.

As a country we are just about maxed out on borrowing, yet every month the government borrows more. And that after nearly six years of austerity. Moreover household debt has risen from 25% of annual disposable income in the 1960s to 150% now. Ever larger amounts of national and personal incomes are required to service these debts, leaving ever less to pay for public services and general living costs.

Interest payments on existing government debt account for more than half the budget deficit. To carry on borrowing is not an option, but to cut the budget deficit without very substantial economic expansion, imposes real hardship upon the weakest and condemns millions to lower standards of living than their parents. This is both unfair and unnecessary. It is an abject failure of a flawed economic model.

The idea for DQE is taken from Treasury banknotes which were issued during WW1 to help fund the cost of the war without excessive borrowing. Up till then only £5 notes had been available, issued mainly by the Bank of England, otherwise money circulating was gold or silver coins. Gold was immediately withdrawn from circulation at the start of the war and the Treasury became responsible for printing all new money in the form of £1 and 10 shilling notes and continued to do so until 1928. So it has been used successfully before. Now, instead of paper, the new money would be electronic.

It was the ending of Treasury control of the money supply and the return to the Gold Standard which occurred in both the US and Britain, which many economists now blame for the Great Depression. Because of misuse of the facility to print money in celebrated historical disasters, there is an irrational fear of doing so.

But money is a measure and a token. It is valueless in isolation unless used to measure wealth or the value of services or goods. Provided printing is for that purpose and properly controlled, it provides the means to expand the economy from the base upwards. Whatever the underlying wealth of a country, it cannot function without sufficient money in circulation in all parts of the economy. Quantitative Easing has restored the financial health of the Establishment and its capital. Dynamic Quantitative Easing will open the prospect of an economic New Deal for the people who hold the country together by their labour.

To sum up

Dynamic Quantitative Easing will

Provide the money to rebalance the economy and create new well paid jobs in infrastructure renewal, rental house building and in local manufacturing for home consumption.

Ease back the value of sterling to create openings for home production of consumables and to boost exports, especially in technology, advanced engineering and motor vehicles.

Secure balanced and sustainable economic growth.

This will result in:

Higher living standards for the majority

Reduced borrowing, closing the balance of payments gap and ending the budget deficit.

Ending the housing shortage.

Ending the need to rely on benefits to boost low incomes and cover excessive housing costs

4

Restoring Democratic Links

The most disturbing aspect of our democracy is that one third of the electorate has voted with its feet. They have given up. There may be many reasons but I intend to highlight three. Each provides Labour with a political opportunity.

New Labour

To cling to the notion that New Labour offers the road to power is to promote, how shall we say, Alice in Wonderland politics. We have already seen in the *Foreword* the extraordinary haemorrhage of votes between 1997 and 2010.

The truth is that once it became clear that New Labour was no longer the champion of the working class and had embraced the priorities of capital above the needs of labour, many walked away. Although some would have wandered off to other parties like the Liberal Democrats, the Greens and later UKIP, the coincidence of falling turnout confirms many stopped voting. But in Scotland in 2015 they returned, not to Labour, but to the anti-austerity left of centre socialist SNP.

Ed Milliband had actually moved away from New Labour intellectually but he was too timid to follow through with a purge of its nostrums. He dropped the New and made a few of the right noises, but his polices remained trapped in the Thatcher consensus and too close to the Tory offer to have real impact. Nevertheless his acknowledgement that his party needed to reconnect to its roots was enough to increase Labour's vote in 2015 for the first time since 1997 and by 100,000 more votes than the increase achieved by the Tories. If the Scottish losses are factored out, the gain in votes in England and Wales is way ahead of the Tories.

The reason for the confusion in the New Labour camp is their belief that voters had turned to them because they had become a centre party. This was not the case. They turned to them because the Major government expired in a suffocating smog of sleaze and division in which a cabinet minister ended up in gaol and the exasperated prime minister, unaware that he was wearing a live microphone, referred to euro-sceptic members of his own cabinet as bastards.

In 1997 the Tories went down to their biggest defeat since the Victorian era, and failed to win a majority for another three elections. Essentially the Conservatives had become unelectable and because of that New Labour succeeded, not out of conviction, but through despair.

Labour has to win back its core votes before it can win another election at Westminster. It may have to accept little support in Scotland, hold its position in Wales and take at least 60 seats off the Tories in England. That is absolutely impossible, now that the Tories are back as a majority party positioned to the left of centre, unless Labour once again connects to those whose interests it was founded to defend. Without those voters who currently stay home it can only win through the weakness of a Tory failure, not by the strength of its own promise.

The Voting System

In 1964, at the General Election, Harold Wilson narrowly won for Labour with 317 seats to the Tories 304. Labour achieved 12.2 million votes. The Tories had 12.0 million. Both seats and votes related to each other. The turnout was 77.1%.

In 2015 the Tories won 11.3 million votes for 330 seats, Labour reached 9.3 million and won 232 seats. So far so good, but look at this. UKIP, the Liberals and the Greens notched up a total of 7.2 million votes, but only won a derisory 10 seats between the lot of them. Yet the SNP won 56 seats on just *1.4* million votes. And Plaid Cymru won 3 seats on a mere 181.6 *thousand* votes, while UKIP got just 1 seat for 3.8 *million* votes.

It is little wonder that disparities on this scale turn people off, because they just see the whole process as rigged. It is not, but first past the post only works if there are two parties in play. If not, a party emerges victorious on a minority of the votes. In Cameron's case he won, but when 63% of the votes were cast against his party. It is said the system produces strong government, but it is at the price of a very weak mandate.

Credibility is not helped by the peculiarities of who can vote for what in the Westminster parliament because of devolution. Nor the fact that following the general election, a total of 45 new peers have been *appointed* to the House Of Lords *for life,* to engage in the legislative process of what is supposed to be a democracy. The list includes famous names caught up in the expenses scandal, others recently thrown out of the Commons by the electorate, and some of whom nobody outside the Westminster village has ever heard.

That reform is required is obvious. There are many different options, including proportional representation, already in use in both the mayoral and devolved assemblies. The minimum threshold is that nobody should be allowed to set foot in either House of Parliament, unless elected to go there by a clear majority of the votes cast, through either transferrable votes or runoff elections. Anything less than that is no longer meeting the gold standard for a modern democracy. Instead it reeks of the rotten practices of an old fashioned fix.

The referendum held in 2011 to decide whether to adopt the Alternative Vote was badly run, with a good deal of misinformation and spin, and settled nothing because the argument was disconnected from the problems it was trying to solve. Indeed there is a good deal of suspicion that the Tories set it up to appease their coalition partners then sabotaged the outcome. There was no constitutional requirement to hold a referendum; any government could readily have introduced a fair voting system, as in mayoral, devolved and EU elections, with a simple Bill in parliament.

Labour will have to come off the fence to put forward a realistic programme for democratic modernisation, including the timely and rapid dissolution of the unelected House of Lords, if it is to have any hope of regaining public trust in its ability to reform. To shelter behind some Royal Commission or Constitutional Convention would be return to the spin doctor's dark art. In today's world of instant communication through social media, which is resistant to spin, that would have no more appeal than a witch doctor's potion. Labour has to demonstrate that it has the ability to come up with good ideas and has the guts to push them through.

What Labour must offer is a renewal of our democracy, clear and unambiguous, in a plan which makes sense, is fair and is fool proof. Then it will win the mandate to carry it out.

The Quango State

Because the people fund the government through taxation, they have a vote to elect the parliament which forms the government. In the past the government was responsible for running the country, so change the government and you changed the way your country was run. That is no longer the case. Huge tracts of government responsibility are now delegated to quangos. Change the government if you want to, but the quangos carry on as before. This creates the impression that voting is pointless.

That is because a gap has opened up between what the people expect and what the politicians deliver. The politicians now judge themselves and each other by how much new legislation they get through parliament. But the voters care little about new laws. They are concerned about how their country is *run*. And most of the running has been delegated to these quangos.

For those unsure of this acronym it means *Quasi-autonomous-non-governmental-organisation.* These words are to most people meaningless. Certainly what meaning they have in this context is misleading. Quasi means not really. Indeed not. These bodies are not autonomous because they are carrying out a function on behalf of the government which pays the cost. The quangos are actually part of the government, but they a cleverly detached from the voters. The buzzword is *independent.*

Until the 1980s various organisations we would now class under the general heading of quango operated successfully and in uncontroversial areas such as the Inland Revenue, and the Forestry Commission. There were more and smaller Ministries in the post war period, each with a minister answerable to parliament. For example there were separate Ministries of Transport, Labour, Education, Civil Aviation, Food, Housing, Fuel and Power etc. Each ministry had a clear remit which was identifiable and a responsibility which it was required to discharge using its own staff and resources. The Ministry of Education had its own school inspectors, for example. In the 1970s reforms created super-ministries, renamed Departments, which combined several different areas of responsibility

As the reshaping of the whole relationship between the State, the economy and the citizen took hold between 1983 and 2010, functions previously the responsibility of ministers directly, were gradually spun off into separate executive agencies to operate at arm's length from government. So we saw the arrival of the Highways Agency in 1994, whereas earlier everything had been under the direct control of the Ministry of Transport. The Civil Aviation Authority replaced the Ministry of Civil aviation as far back as 1972.

What really drove big changes was the Thatcher programme of privatisation, because this required a whole new set of regulators to control what had previously been mostly state monopolies. The driver of privatisation was the failure to modernize and invest in the nationalised industries during the troubled seventies and the government did not want to borrow on the scale required at the prevailing high interest rates. Private companies would have access to more competitive finance. There was also the political view that the power of the trade unions would be reduced and a wider shareholding public would be more likely to vote Tory. Thatcher was a gifted political opportunist.

However, there was a fear that private monopolies would run amok and become a political liability, so the idea of regulators to control them was dreamed up. The notion was that these regulators would be independent of government and work within the legal definitions under which they had been set up. Some regulated price, some quality, some both. According to the Government information website there are 24 Ministerial Departments (which we used to call ministries) but there are another 22 Non Ministerial Departments. Essentially these represent the visible apex of a vast quango iceberg.

Some of the non-ministerial departments like the Crown Prosecution Service are obviously in the public interest. But what about the Office for Rail and Road? Have you heard of that? Perhaps not. But you are paying for it. This is what it says it does.

The Office of Rail and Road (ORR) is the independent safety and economic regulator for Britain's railways and monitor of Highways England. It is responsible for ensuring that railway operators comply with health and safety law. It regulates Network Rail's activities and funding requirements, regulates access to the railway network, licenses the operators of railway assets and publishes rail statistics. ORR is also the competition authority for the railways and enforces consumer protection law in relation to the railway. As highways monitor ORR is responsible for monitoring Highways England's management of the strategic road network – the motorways and main 'A' roads in England.

But wait a minute. *Highways England* is a government Agency and Network Rail is a not for profit company limited by guarantee in which the only member is the Secretary of State for Transport. There is a question over the notion of quangos, but there is none over the principle of quangos on top of quangos in a mad hatter's pyramid. That is absurd.

The NHS has 26 quangos or whatever you want to call them in a spider's web of bureaucratic intricacies so confusing that memoranda of understanding have had to be drawn up to discover who does what. This is how the responsibilities are described on Monitor's website in respect of its relationship to the Care Quality Commission.

CQC and Monitor have distinct but complementary roles. Monitor is the independent regulator of NHS foundation trusts (FTs). It assesses whether NHS trusts can become FTs, regulates FTs and makes sure they are run well on behalf of patients and taxpayers. Under the Health and Social Care Act, Monitor will continue this until 2016.

CQC registers all providers of health and adult social care regulated activities, and requires them to meet essential standards of quality and safety. Monitor will license a sub-set of these providers (those who provide NHS-funded services) and require them to follow certain behaviours relating to price setting, integrated care, competition and ensuring service continuity if a provider gets into financial difficulties

You can make of this what you will, but anyone who has ever run anything from a village jumble sale to a multinational corporation will know that this is no way to do it and more particularly so if it is being done with taxpayer's money. The counter argument is that because taxpayer's money is involved you have to have these idiotic structures. The knockout blow is that because taxpayer's money is involved you cannot afford to have them, because they divert money from its real purpose. If Foundation Hospitals can only be run subject to this outlandish rigmarole, they should be forthwith brought back under the direct control of the Department of Health, who should appoint a Manager (not a chief executive) to run each one and get on with their core task of treating the sick.

Moreover because public money is being used, the direct line to the democratic process via the minister through parliament must be short and responsive and without any ambiguity or fudging. First the minister is fired by the government and if that does not work, the government is fired by the people.

That is what democracy is. It may not be the most efficient form of government but it is the fairest and it cannot be turned into some arm's length independent process detached from voters whose preferences have either no effect or one so diluted that they are not even aware of it. Because if that happens they will stop voting. And they have. In 2015 some 16 million who had troubled to register stayed at home.

There is a place for a few Executive Agencies in a well-balanced democracy, but it is wrong for the functions of democratic government to be delegated to bodies outside democratic control. This leads to the gradual introduction of a form of soft autocracy which, although notionally subject to democratic sanction, in practice is outside it.

In the worst cases, and the NHS is probably the worst of all, it leads to incredible structures which defy comprehension and an entire army of management managing not events and outcomes, but the performance of itself and each other.

New Labour is as guilty of setting up this spider's web of public management as the Tories. It is a joint enterprise and people are fed up with it. It sucks energy and resources into a mad world of monitors monitoring monitors and a fraudulent and dishonest pretence that all these organisations are endowed with an independence they should not have. They are, if they are needed at all, part of the public structure of accountable government and responsible to the people.

We must finally look at the advent of a new type of Shareholder Corporation, invented by the Tories, but nurtured and expanded by New Labour. This is the outsourcing of basic services previously provided by public employees working for the government, local authorities and public institutions of all kinds. Some of the companies involved have customers in the private sector, some do not. They usually take on the public employees as their own, but with little job security and often with low wages which have to be subsidised by tax credits and housing benefit. The programme has accelerated under the Tory led coalition, but New Labour kept it alive enthusiastically. Huge sums are paid to these privately owned publicly funded companies; by 2014 the Coalition had spent £90 billion on them, ranging from school cleaners to running prisons and more recently the probation service.

One contact I discovered for educational support services, awarded to a well-known corporation which seems to do this kind of thing as a core activity, was for *twenty years*. You cannot operate public policy involving services as if you are giving a ground lease on a property. Moreover there is massive public investment in the private sector for the benefit of shareholders entirely beyond the control of taxpayers. The claim that money is saved is false. It always is in the first year or two, but after that the service deteriorates and the public gets a bad deal far too often.

There may be just a few cases where some kind of partnership is appropriate, but not many. Because the rule must be that if public money pays the bill, it must be for public, not shareholder benefit, and fully accountable through the democratic process by a direct line which the voters can see and act upon.

Public employees who are properly paid, have job security and work for their country knowing that it will never make them rich, are a precious national asset, not a liability. Functions which are paid for by taxpayers should not be awarded to private companies for the profit of shareholders. The argument is that in spite of the need to pay dividends, the private sector delivers better value than the public sector. First, if this is the case over the long term which mostly it is not, it is at the price of lower standards, lower pay and less secure working conditions. Second, and this is the nub, if the money comes from taxpayers, it must remain in the public sector under democratic control. This is the difference between public and private.

A private sector paid out of public funds is a misuse of enterprise and diverts energy from innovation and wealth creation, which is the front line role of business. A public sector which contacts out its services to private business loses control of public money which it is its duty to manage and protect.

Restoring proper democratic accountability so that the responsibility for running the country is taken back to the government should be a priority in the next Labour manifesto. There are 16 million extra votes to be harvested as a reward.

5

Responsibility of Government.

It is a fantasy to suppose that an economy based on house price inflation and debt fuelled consumption of imported goods is going anywhere other than to another crash. It is also unrealistic to imagine that some way will be found to reduce imports and increase exports with the pound in its present state of over valuation.

Until there is a fundamental change of the economic model in the UK from one dominated by services, shopping and borrowing to one which creates new wealth by investing in manufacturing and technology both for home consumption and for competitive exports and can drive sustained growth, there is no way that any of the aspirations of any political party to reduce poverty, improve services, end the housing crisis, or reduce the gap between rich and poor will be met.

Prosperity derived from a much bigger contribution to fundamental wealth creation is the only way to finally see off austerity and create a fair tax base sufficient to meet the demands of a modern welfare state. Because the base of the economy is short of money and creates little to none on its own, it contributes too little to the revenue stream to guarantee that costs of the services and welfare needs can be readily met. So there are cuts and shortages. This creates social tensions and intolerance towards minorities and immigrants, because of strains on basic necessities like health, education and housing.

The markets have led the UK economy into one of the most dangerous regions of economic peril, fuelled by Tory reforms nurtured by New Labour. Debt per household is at historic highs and the cost of servicing these debts takes an ever larger share of every household budget. We make a tiny proportion of what we consume and import the rest. Not only is the economic model unsustainable but the detached style of management of it is a complete political failure.

What is now required to rescue the country is not just a protest movement, although protests are right and will grow, but a clear and coherent plan to re-establish the process of creating new wealth from investment, rather than asset inflation through borrowing.

This will require sustained economic growth of not less than 5% per year for several years. That will never be achieved by leaving the markets in charge. A Labour government will have to buck the trend and restore political control to the levers of economic power.

Rebooting the manufacture of most of what we consume is necessary to create the opportunities for skilled and rewarding employment for the rising generation. We have to restore to positive our balance of trade through cutting imports and increasing competitive exports. We must spread prosperity more widely, reducing the gap between rich and poor. Wealth has to be created by all for the benefit of all, not by some for the benefit of the few, and especially not at the expense of the poorest.

We have explored the impact of government through statutory bodies and its effects on reducing accountability to the electorate. The contention is that full democracy may not be efficient, but it is fair and is the only way to engage properly the human right of the sovereignty of the people. The most critical area where a democratic government should control all the levers of power, is the economy. Globalisation has led to a drift of economic power from government to central bank and in our case, to the Bank of England. The notion is that government retains control of policy while the Bank manages the consequences.

In practice a subtle reversal occurs. The Bank ends up controlling the shape and balance of the economy and the government is left with organising the distribution. In the present terms of the UK, the government is engaged in a cutting programme because the economy has been unable to deliver all the recourses necessary to maintain public services and welfare at the optimum level. This is said to be either the fault of a previous government, which is just not supported by even a casual look at the figures, or upon global forces outside the government's control.

This is wrong. The problem is that the financial model is one which cannot deliver the kind of economy people expect, because it is out of the control of both the people and the government; it has been given away to market forces. Market forces are not like the weather. They are manmade. They are a great engine of human advancement, but like any engine, they must be wisely driven. Driverless they always end in a crash.

Between 1945 and 1972 there was no serious recession in the UK economy. This was a world of exchange controls, fixed currency values and pretty rigorous control by the Treasury (the government) of almost every detail of economic management, including from time to time but not very successfully, pay. The doubling of the oil price in 1973 as a consequence of the Arab–Israeli War had a devastating effect on the certainties underlying the UK economy which then produced no oil, resulting in financial turmoil, which continued in various forms for the rest of the 1970s and was the catalyst which gave rise to what we call Thatcherism.

Conservative chancellors progressively unravelled the whole structure of government controls over the economy, believing that the markets knew best. Surprisingly it was New Labour which delivered the *coup de grace* when it gave responsibility for interest rates and inflation to the Bank of England. The belief was that, freed from political interference, the economy would provide a smoother ride with less boom and bust. All seemed good until we ran into arguably the biggest bust in history. This was not really surprising, although everybody seemed to be taken by surprise at the time.

There will always be an economic cycle in a modern industrialised economy, which does not vary in concept if the economy is global. If the cycle is left to the markets to self-adjust, the booms will last longer and reach greater heights, but the busts will be deeper and last longer as well. We are still trying to recover after 2007/8 and remain gripped by austerity in public services and welfare. So the boom and bust did not go away. Unfortunately these longer spans have meant that one generation gains and the next loses out and may never be able to gain parity with those who orchestrated the bust. This breeds resentment and social discord.

It is to some extent true that a central bank has the tools at its disposal, but there is an element of dysfunction because many, if not most, of the decisions called for have options from which to choose and many choices are political. The Bank has to be above politics, which leads to inaction, or action which is prudent financially but arbitrary in effect. Thus the financial sector recovered much faster than the basic economy, following the crash.

Moreover during the run up to the crash a processes begun in the Thatcher era accelerated to create our misshapen economic model, unable to deliver the taxation volume to sustain services and modernise the infrastructure. Debt became almost a second currency and assets, especially housing, accelerated in value way ahead of inflation, while manufacturing and industry declined.

For historical rather than financial reasons sterling is overvalued in relation to the fundamentals of modern Britain. This sucks in imports which are cheaper than home production. It kills exports which become uncompetitive. Skilled jobs are exported and replaced with low wage employment in the retail or service sectors.

There is very little that the government can do about any of this, because modern governments no longer control the levers of financial power. It can be argued that they used them badly when they had them, so they were passed to safer hands. The reality is they passed to dead hands and that has created a whole new set of live problems. One of the most acute is the fact that financial markets naturally suck wealth from the base to the top. To ensure markets operate for the common good, a delicate political counterbalance is needed. In modern Britain that is now missing.

New Labour was happy to embrace the notion of this detached approach to economic management and in so doing abandoned the interests of the people it was supposed to look after, which is one of the explanations of several for the loss of millions of votes during its ascendancy. Labour will now have to think about all this and decide what to do. It will have to come forward with a modern design in order to demonstrate that it has a grip of current economic realities and can be trusted to use the tools wisely for the benefit of the many on whom the functioning of the nation depends.

The ideas on the table must include, in addition to Dynamic Quantitative Easing, the restoration to government of the political levers of economic power, to enable it to reshape the economy so as to deliver growth and revenue and restore prosperity. This must include control over interest rates, including mortgages, personal borrowing and savings, the supply of money to the basic economy and a pro-active approach to the value of sterling.

The Bank of England must be engaged as a major source of advice, but its responsibility should be removed from political judgements and concentrated on maintaining the integrity of the banking and financial systems. If necessary its powers should be enhanced to enable it to discharge that critical function, although after the recent upgrade of City regulation generally, this should not be necessary.

Inflation is now more global than local and is often driven by events outside national control. Nevertheless rash national policies such as increasing the money supply too sharply leading to a shortage of materials, skills and labour could easily create a problem. Therefore responsibility must ultimately rest with government. Politicians cannot absent themselves from key decisions concerning core financial issues such as interest rates, house price inflation, household debt and currency value. The Labour plan should include restoration of political control over:

Interest Rates

Inflation

The Money Supply at all levels of the economy

Policies which affect the value of the currency, which initially must move downwards.

Direct Funding of infrastructure modernization, affordable housing, cheaper energy for industry and business, and world beating e-communications in all regions.

6

Taxation

Over the years our taxation system has become far too complicated. It has also been demonised by the right and used as a weapon by the left. It needs simplifying and rebranding not as a burden, but a means of empowerment and a foundation for growth. A whole industry has grown up dedicated to avoiding tax and is a lot more successful than the countermeasures set up by successive governments to thwart it. It is time for a rethink. The system is too complex to administer without great cost and it should be simplified. This is not a suitable platform to argue taxation reform in depth, but it is possible to sketch out some thoughts.

It is time to accept that the deficit problems of the UK are as much about too little revenue as they are about too much expenditure. The answer lies in having the right sort of taxes, effective in a modern globalised world. We must stop obsessing about tax rates. These should be seen as fine tuning at the margin, not as a political weapon. A quick look at some simple figures illustrates the point. In the tax year 2010/11 forward projections were issued which indicted in 2014/15 the total revenue would reach £597 billion. It actually came in at £515 billion. The difference is the deficit. Tax income had not grown sufficiently.

First something needs to be done about the image. Taxation is seen as a bad thing to be avoided. Yet if you were to tell the very people who complain about tax that they are going to be charged in the NHS for seeing a GP or a visit to A&E, that Trident will be abandoned and the country's borders opened, because it all costs too much, then those same people will go ballistic. Taxation is a good thing because it enables all the securities of a safe and caring country. But to be accepted it has to be simple, fair and effective.

At present it is none of these things and especially with modern international corporations, it often fails to produce any meaningful revenue. In the tax year 2014/2015 (the latest figures at time of writing) the actual revenue generated by all business taxes, including bank levies etc., was only 9% of total tax receipts. This is just not a big enough contribution for all the business activity in the country.

The case for change is overwhelming. With globalisation it is just too easy for multinationals to fix things so that tax falls due in a completely different jurisdiction to the one in which the money is earned. Too much of what is actually collected comes from SMEs who do not have access to tax avoidance options, with too little flowing from big business and much too little from global giants.

The two most successful elements of mainstream taxation are PAYE and VAT. Both are based on cash flow rather than profit. Profit and the jurisdiction in which the head office of a corporation is situated affect the amount owing under the law, sometimes by hundreds of millions if not billions. The way to deal with this is to eliminate profit as a factor for business taxes and change to a turnover tax, collected on every pound received by any business within the UK, irrespective of where its head office or its tax domicile is.

Corporation tax should be abolished and with it the hugely expensive taxation avoidance industry, since turnover tax would be unavoidable. Tax would become a first charge overhead, just as it is for those on

PAYE, and would be no different to the energy bill. It would be sensible to eliminate the separate NI contribution paid by employers and include the contribution in the turnover tax.

To protect small businesses the first, say, £100,000 of turnover in a year could be tax free. Their owners and the self-employed generally would pay PAYE on their personal drawings and benefits in kind. Although the rate of a turnover tax would be much lower than corporation tax, the revenue would be much larger because the spread would be wider and avoidance, short of fraud, impossible.

There is a strong argument for Basic Rate of income tax and for national insurance contributions to be morphed into a new combination called National Welfare Contribution. This would be paid on all incomes from whatever source and however big, above a personal allowance level of £14,000. I do not want to talk about rates in this context, as to arrive at accurate conclusions would require data and software available to professional economists. Probably a combined rate would be in the region of 25% (Thatcher's basic rate). Higher rate tax, currently 45% could be renamed Higher Income Contribution and would be quoted as an addition. At an addition of 20% the combination would remain at 45%.

Finally capital gains tax needs to be abolished. Over the years it has been revised and tinkered with and much time and expense is involved both in collecting and avoiding it. It should be replaced with a universal Capital Transaction Tax. This would be payable on all capital transactions, including shares and property, irrespective of gains or losses. It would be based on the gross sum and split evenly between buyer and seller. Stamp duty would go.

To summarise, these proposals shift taxation away from accounting processes which can be argued over and challenged, towards the basic flow of money. Tax then falls either on money in or money out. There are no loopholes and the collection process is both cleaner and more complete. The tax base is much wider, therefore the rates can be lower. The burden is directly related to ability to pay, the poorest pay the least, the richest the most, the largest corporations cannot escape; everybody contributes. And that is what taxation is. It is the mandatory contribution to ensure a fully functioning state. There is nothing more important for human society than that. We now know only too well what happens when states fail.

What is needed is a simple system, which is seen to be fair, that collects tax from a wider base, spreads the load more evenly and increases revenue. This must be set at levels sufficient to pay fully all the bills of a modern advanced welfare economy and provide the kind of financial platform to build prosperity for all.

7

Reconnecting Labour to Power

It is necessary to bite the bullet and begin this chapter with a lot of negatives, starting with New Labour. In 1997, after 18 years of the Thatcher revolution the Tories were clapped out, split and sleaze ridden. The predictable landslide came from disillusioned Tories as much as from fired up Labour supporters. Tony Blair led a government with wide and deep public support. It believed this support stemmed from its abandonment of socialism, its semi-detachment from the Labour Movement and its spin that it was a party of the centre, a teeny bit left, which would embrace most of Thatcher's nostrums. Indeed one of the first public acts of the new prime minister was to invite her to tea.

Thereafter New Labour followed the Thatcherite tradition and made no fundamental changes to the new economic settlement which her governments had inaugurated. Blair's high achievements were the Good Friday Agreement, devolution for Scotland and Wales, restoration of City government in London through an elected mayor, equalities legislation, the Human

Rights Act and the emergence of a more caring society.

The failures were strategic and glaring. No attempt was made to curb house price inflation, arrive at a clear plan to maintain the country's energy needs and generating capacity, or formulate a programme to renew social housing. There was a complete failure to revitalise industry and exports. Domination by markets was encouraged and the gap between rich and poor grew. And let us not forget Iraq.

New Labour distanced itself from its roots and became semi- detached from the Labour movement as a whole. The working classes, seeing that they were all but abandoned by their champion, walked away in large numbers, especially the young. The catalyst came in Scotland, where the original Labour party took root. There, a new left wing modern socialist party, the SNP, grew and grew and although it failed in its bid to achieve Scottish independence, it wiped New Labour from the Scottish political map at the general election in 2015. In England a revived left leaning Tory party and a working class friendly UKIP thwarted the Labour attack.

The outcome is that Labour now has just one seat in Scotland and over ninety seats fewer than the Tories in England. To get within sight of power, let alone achieve it, might now be all but out of reach for Labour for a generation; the more so if it for one second supposes that this will be by the road of sucking up to business and going to cocktail parties with the filthy rich.

But there is a way. It is a political change of weather amounting to a social revolution. It is fired by passion, commitment and energy because it is driven by the young. The young are tired of getting a deal at the start of their adult lives which falls far short of the offer to their parents. There is something deeply cynical about the remnants of what is called the centre ground, with its pervading inequalities, lacklustre economy and ballooning debt.

The young know it does not have to be like this and if Labour can show it has answers which are fresh and full of promise of fairer, better, times, it can sweep again to power with a mandate to reform on the scale of 1945. Although Labour is currently holding 232 seats against the Tory total of 331, this is a lot better than the starting line-up faced by

Clement Atlee. He had 152 to the Tory 473, yet he won a landslide mandate for the inauguration of the Welfare State.

What Labour now has to do is to prepare a comprehensive reboot of the whole economic settlement which, while informed by history, does not revert to the past. Rather it advances to a brighter future by restoring the dynamism of the industrial economy and the accountability of the democratic process. As set out already this should include:

This combination of reforms would enable Labour to lead the political conversation in the run up to the 2020 general election. This will require a radical programme which will inspire the young and re-energise Labour supporters who have drifted away or become non-voters during the New Labour era. To win big, Labour will have to launch a targeted campaign upon their principle opponents, the Tories, and put them on the back foot from the very beginning. Ghosting them will not work.

To achieve a majority in England, Labour has to drive a stake through the Tory electoral heart. It can do this, but before we examine how, we must take a closer look at the key dynamics of politics in England today. England is the key because Labour cannot win a majority any longer unless it wins in England.

The SNP is not likely to collapse in Scotland and although Labour may improve on its current single seat, there would have to be some much unexpected political developments to put it back into the 40s. Politics is notoriously difficult to predict, but plans must be laid on realistic assumptions. Although there have been expectations that we were moving towards multi party politics, this can only happen in the regions or cities where proportional electoral systems are in place.

For the Westminster parliament, as long as first past the post remains, it is the relationship between the two big parties which will dominate the outcome. Third parties in England only make a little headway if there are issues which motivate enough marginal voters in key areas. This happened to the Liberal Democrats during the New Labour era, when the Tories were seen as too far to the right in the south and New Labour not left enough in the north. The high profile interventions in 2015 of a fourth party, UKIP, and a fifth option, the Greens, was a disaster to the Lib Dems and they ended up with just 8 seats.

The plain truth is that first past the post has two effects. One is that it ensures that a party without an electoral majority in percentage terms will gain a parliamentary majority as long as it gets more votes translated into seats than its nearest rival. The other is that two parties will always dominate, split between capital and labour. It is on this basis that Labour has to fight in 2020 and it cannot win unless it defeats the establishment party of capital in England. It will not do that on the strength of its own manifesto alone. It has to destroy the image and the confidence of its opponent.

In the history of the Labour Movement only three party leaders have ever won a majority. Attlee offered a new social and economic settlement. Wilson offered to harness the white heat of the technological revolution. Blair offered to make a difference from a Tory government in power for eighteen years which was split, seedy and exhausted.

In 2020 the Tory party could be on the ropes, because in politics you can never be sure. But it may very well be flying high, so high that it will be confident nothing can bring it down. We know that unlike Labour's three winning leaders since 1930, the Tories have had nine who have won and they will have a new leader determined to make it ten in 2020. Make no mistake, whatever its euphoria under its popular new leader, Labour is approaching its Henry the Fifth moment in 2020.

To achieve victory Labour will have to unravel the Tory claim to economic competence and demonstrate that the party of the establishment is working against the people. The soundbite should be that the Tories have become the party of debt. Personal debt, corporate debt, government debt. They cannot generate enough income to balance the books without cutting benefits to the poorest and borrowing to top up. They have nurtured an economic model which effectively enslaves, through excessive housing costs and low wages, almost the whole working class to borrowing to get a roof to live under and then more borrowing again to keep going. This leaves little over, which is not committed to one or other financial institution.

And these financial institutions are almost all owned by the Tories and their supporters. The whole structure at the top of the economy, which bears down heaviest on those least able to cope, is designed to suck money from the base to the top and it is the Tories who built it this way. The well-off prosper while the single parents struggle. The ever burgeoning financial services industries offer all manner of money making careers to professionals and their acolytes, but create little if any new wealth beyond the inflation of assets.

The whole thing depends on the ever growing flow of borrowing and payments, subsidised by the state in the form of necessary housing benefit and working tax credits, which is hobbling a whole generation forced to set out into adult life without any of the prospects enjoyed by their parents. Indeed those who have made the effort to go to university, graduate already in debt to the tune of nearly £60,000. At every level profit is being made by the richer at the expense of the poorer, who can no longer afford to save, and are forced to clamber onto the notorious housing ladder, in order to aim for some degree of security. And that ensures the whole pernicious system keeps churning upwards.

There is no chance for ordinary people to redress this balance as there are so few skilled jobs being created by the promised re-birth of industry, which cannot happen because the currency is over-valued and the base of the economy is starved of new money and relies on debt. And who benefits from the high currency and cheap imports and debt which reflect in high asset values? Yes you do not need a prompt. The Tory governing establishment.

They miss all their economic targets and try to run vital public services on a shoestring, which they claim is necessary to solve the problem. But the truth is the Tories and all they have come to stand for *are* the problem and the way to solve it is to get rid of their government. In so doing, victorious Labour can change the political weather to a more energised country in which increasing prosperity brought about by industrial revival is more widely shared. A nation modernised and inclusive, which values the contribution of all its citizens at every level and gives them a fair deal, in which you can get rich by creating new wealth, but never by siphoning money from those least able to afford it.

That is why Labour has to gain power. The foregoing offers some ideas of how this can be done. The headings are:

Reboot the economy using £375 billion of Dynamic Quantitative Easing over a Parliament, plus a reduction in the value of sterling. Both these must take place irrespective of the position of the economic cycle. <u>It must also happen whether Britain stays in or leaves the EU and whether Scotland remains part of the UK or goes it alone.</u>

Cut the proliferation of agencies and quangos wherever possible using smaller more focused ministries responsible to parliament and the electorate.

Restore government authority over financial policy including the currency and interest rates. This will reverse the drift of power towards the establishment, and restore it to the people. It will also enable the government to influence markets rather than simply follow them.

End the housing crisis by building two million homes to rent on long tenancies at affordable rents.

Introduce taxation reform which switches taxation from situations to money flow, making avoidance impossible except through fraud, which would be a criminal, not a civil, offence. This will both increase revenue and eventually reduce rates because of a much wider taxation base.

8

Rebooting the Nation

If it is to win, Labour has to put meaningful proposals to the electorate which, in my view, should be based on the ideas for reform in this narrative. This will enable Labour to engage the pent up energy, especially among the young, for a complete reboot of the economic settlement which has created such a dispiriting style of centre politics driven by self-interest. Markets, globalisation, getting on, the right thing, are all buzz phrases to excuse the ever growing power of the strong over the weak. And as always happens when this cycle of greed becomes entrenched, the strong grow fewer but ever more powerful and the rest grow ever weaker as their numbers swell.

Indeed their weakness is portrayed as getting on. But the reality is that families where parents work round the clock to sustain excessive housing costs, childcare costs, often borrowing to make ends meet on zero hours contracts, are not really getting on at all. They are stuck with the fruits of their effort being sucked up into that overbearing financial structure which dominates everything. That is the politics of the centre.

To change the political weather and restore prosperity in depth, which is fairly shared, Labour not only has to win, but it has to win *real power*. It will never do that from the centre, because the centre is a power vacuum for government, which is why the establishment loves it. Labour has to win from the *Left*.

Attlee won from the left and so did Wilson. Thatcher won from the right, because the left had become economically dysfunctional. Just as Attlee had shifted the centre to the left, creating a new political weather, so she shifted it to the right and did likewise. Blair was able to win from that centre, because of the lack of electoral appeal of the worn out Tory party, not because of the emotional appeal of Labour. It also won because Thatcherism remained the prevailing political choice and New Labour was clearly Thatcherite.

There is now so much wrong with the centre at every level of policy that although an election *could* be won from there if all parties were positioned there and it was the only option, it would be a disaster for the country. It would not only leave the flawed economic model with its mounting social problems unchecked, it would empower the Far Right. A left win is historically necessary.

Labour has to come forward with a comprehensive agenda for a new deal across the whole spectrum of public policy; just tinkering with taxation rates to make the rich pay more would be futile. The challenges of creating such a manifesto are considerable but doable; the challenges of winning and putting promises into reality will be even more demanding. So it seems right to end with a check list of the toughest areas, where the promise must be credible and the implementation effective.

Labour has three areas of weakness among floating and non-voters; the economy, the deterrent and the trade unions. It has two strengths; social housing and the NHS. Let us look at these electoral strengths first.

NHS

Labour invented the NHS and has always been seen as its friend. The Tories have to work hard to convince voters that they are not meddling with it just to cut costs. There are now mounting signs that cuts and so called efficiency savings are beginning to affect the quality of patient care; a situation made worse by the quango ridden management structure and disjointed application of healthcare between separate authorities, boards and services.

Labour will have to come forward with a simplification of how it is run and a coherent way of funding it. Neither the structure nor the funding is any longer fit for purpose and any offer of a New Labour style makeover will be trampled at election time under Tory feet. Three things must happen. A new funding system which expands as demand grows is essential. It is mathematically impossible to provide an infinite service on a finite budget. At the moment the more patients who use the NHS the greater the strain on the cash. And this will get worse and worse.

Next, this is a twenty-four seven service. Therefore hospitals should never close. They should be open round the clock, full services operational on three eight hour shifts. Operations could be done day and night. Waiting lists would be eliminated along with the costly administration that they require. All the quangos would also go and a simplified management structure with the Secretary of State, head on the block, directly responsible through national, regional and district managers, tasked to manage healthcare not each other. This is a publicly funded service not an arm's length contractor and the shambolic combination of trusts, foundations, boards and authorities is a waking nightmare of idiotic empire building which has to stop.

Third, doctors should be directly employed, all of them, by the NHS, to work full time for the service with normal working hours and decent conditions which will allow a comfortable life of quality and integrity, but which will not make them rich, because medicine is not that sort of vocation. Moonlighting into private practice by culling waiting lists to see better off or insured patients privately up the road and fix their problems, while the NHS waiting list for the same doctor grows, in morally appalling. Doctors who want to do that leave the NHS and immediately repay in full the cost of training a replacement at the current level and indexed for inflation; starting at a baseline of £350,000.

Labour founded the NHS. It is time to reclaim it for the people. They pay for it.

Social Housing

New Labour's housing record is disappointing but there is public trust that Labour is now more energised to set things right. The Blair and Brown governments should have intervened at the very beginning to replace and expand the housing stock denuded by Thatcher's right to buy. Failure has led to a housing crisis which has warped the economy, increased household debt beyond sustainable levels, inflated house prices beyond reason and forced the government to subsidise the rent of millions charged by private landlords many times what they themselves can afford. Tory private landlords. Remember that. Private landlords made rich on public money. Not only that but the various Tory schemes to help first time buyers with loan guarantees and deposit help, are actually inflating house prices even further. That was the intention, although they will deny it.

The solution is simple if challenging. Build two million new affordable homes at rents which people can pay without subsidy on long tenancies which do not involve the need or the right to purchase. Either to be owned by local authorities in the traditional format or by a new National Housing Authority. All state owned, private contractors only for construction, funded by DQE for the public good. This should be the first public investment programme announced by an incoming Labour government.

Now we must concentrate on the key electoral weaknesses.

Trade Unions

The Trade Unions are where old Labour, in the sense of the Labour Movement, came to electoral grief. The New Labour era was, as previously asserted in this narrative, a continuation of Thatcherism dressed in pink.

Labour is not a party, it is a Movement. It is a movement inaugurated to offer a democratic counter-balance to the power of the Establishment which champions the interests of capital. The Labour Movement challenges that perspective of the economic and social structure and presents an alternative power base, founded on the interests of the working people or labour with a small *l*. It was this alternative power base which was the driving force of politics from the end of WWII to the advent of Thatcher.

The Trade Unions are the living core of the Labour Movement without which the Movement ceases to be; they are also a vital source of finance. Their public profile fell into disrepute as the 1970s advanced, because their power was used politically to topple the Heath government, after which there followed a Labour government bedevilled with industrial relations out of control and an economy in serious decline. This resulted in eighteen years of Tory government, halving of trade union membership, decimation of the UK's industrial base and a good deal of reform of the legal framework under which unions function.

The first thing to say is that the way forwards is not backwards. The unions have undertaken very significant remodelling of the offer they make to their members and industrial relations are better than they have ever been. Nevertheless too many people who could benefit from union membership shun the opportunity because they have no personal inclination to strike and if they live in the South East, are tired of union disputes making them late for work.

Additionally New Labour became semi-detached from the unions and, as a consequence of that, the Movement lost cohesion and diverged so that the political link with the working classes was undermined. The new leader from the left, elected with a huge popular mandate, struggles to unite a parliamentary party which is far to the right of both its leader and its membership. A period of political turbulence is likely and this makes it all the more important for the synergy between the unions and the party to be re-established.

A way forward for the collective unions working through the TUC would be to play a more proactive role in the financial health of their members. Before deregulation the whole country was covered in building societies, friendly societies, credit unions and mutual insurance companies which acted not only as a source of funding and saving for working people, but as a financial balance to the weight of the City. Now everything to do with money is centralised and concentrated to maximise shareholder profit and establishment power, while the payday loan industry, with its eye popping interest rates, preys upon the insecurity of low paid workers, who struggle to meet costs beyond their means.

Unions could trigger a rebirth, in modern form online, of banking, insurance and other mutual financial firms, friendly to the needs of modern working people. Harnessing the saving and investment potential of their membership would create a significant financial platform. In return they will not only present an upgraded membership offer relevant to the way the modern world has developed, but can realistically demand the introduction of German style supervisory boards with equal union representation.

Another area where action is needed to overcome the skills shortage is in education. People lament the end of the grammar school era, but it is the shortage of the high quality skills training in the secondary moderns and the support of the technical colleges which has had a much more serious economic impact. Union sponsorship of Academies giving modern high quality vocational secondary education, a modern version of technical colleges and sponsorship of apprenticeships would be of great value. It brings the unions right into the centre of the national endeavour so that instead of being associated, however unfairly, with disputes and strikes, they become an acknowledged engine of economic growth.

To win in 2020 at a level to empower it to carry out major reform, will require a significant consensus among the electorate that the Labour Movement has answers to the problems which bedevil their lives. This must include a programme to reindustrialize our economy and inaugurate substantial and sustainable growth over a period of years. Where Britain is weak industrially is not in the big areas like defence, aerospace or automotives, but on consumer products which fill our shops and stores. Almost all this stuff is imported. It is fine to have a consumer economy but to squander the opportunity it produces for home manufacturing, is an economic car crash which has to be remedied. For that there will have to be a bold plan.

Central to the credibility of that plan is the need for the Unions to be in the vanguard of it. That would trigger the attraction of new members. The initial target would be to return to the ten million level. That can be achieved by the restoration of the TUC's self-confidence and a modern, inspiring membership offer, upgraded to the tests and trials of the economic environment in which working people now find themselves. When the Labour Movement is united and strong, promoting a bold plan of action to right the wrongs of favouring the few by exploiting the many, which is what the Tory debt driven economy has done, it wins. And it wins big.

The Deterrent

New Labour was every bit as hawkish as, and started more wars than, the Tories. But there is a widespread belief that traditional Labour is soft on defence; in particular it is thought to be against the nuclear deterrent. The leadership certainly is, the trade unions are divided and the new mass of members and supporters are probably by a majority against renewing Trident. To reach a balanced conclusion (unless as a matter of principle you are opposed no matter what), it seems to me that one must first do two things. Look a little more closely at what a rational and proactive foreign policy might look like and, in addition, what these weapons actually are and what they can do. It is then possible to have a better determination of potential threats and assess the suitability of the systems needed to deter them.

Before I go further I must share with you my own background, which pulls me to stand back and take a detached, rather than nationalistic view of world affairs. I am British, but of my four grandparents, three were German by birth. Two became British, one born British became German and then became, with her husband and daughter (my mother, who was born in Africa) American. One great-grandmother was Jewish as well as German and two English great grandparents were killed in the Blitz in 1940. My second wife was American and two of my children are dual US/UK nationals but have a Norwegian grandmother. My eldest daughter is dual Australian/British. My grandchildren are Australian, but two thirds of the blood in their veins is a mix of Polish and German. So when I think about international affairs, I see first the world and then my country. Most people see the opposite.

Economically Britain follows a fairly independent line when determining its policy overseas, but on diplomacy and military issues it is so close to the US that many regard the two countries as tantamount to one. There are historic reasons for this which in the short narrative of this book we have no need to explore. What can be said is that America is much less sure footed post cold war than during it and that post 9/11 there have been catastrophic errors of judgement which have led to an awful lot of unnecessary killing and suffering. Britain, or its governments, still sees itself as a strategic power. But it can only play the part because of its close attachment to US policy of power projection.

Since the Cold War ended America has been unable to move on from the doctrine of confrontation, left over from the Nazi and Communist eras. It may well be that it sees that as the best way forward to protect and promote its interests. It may also be that Pentagon influence encourages a posture of vast military expenditure which has to be justified.

The main destabilising feature of the post-cold war period has been the continuous eastward expansion of NATO into an organisation which bears little resemblance to its origin, even though its potential enemy, the Warsaw Pact, no longer exists. Added to that is the disproportionate military budget of the US, which spends more than all the other military powers in the world put together. Instead of making the world safer, this actually makes it more dangerous, because the expansion creates the very challenges which it is inaugurated to deter.

There are two ways of looking at what comes next. The first is that Britain and America are closer together than any other powers on earth. Their intelligence and defence systems are intertwined, as are their economies and corporations. Looked at from afar they appear two independent countries but one nation. Britain is the junior partner in size and wealth, but punches well above its weight on the world stage because of its close ties with the world's richest, most powerful and assertive country. America is always more confident if Britain is there beside it.

This presents Britain with enormous advantages, but it poses a significant strategic risk. An aggressor may calculate that eliminating America's principal ally in a nuclear strike would not be sufficient to cause the US to trigger its own destruction by retaliating and would therefore be willing to do a deal to save mankind. Remember the only time it may pay to use nuclear weapons is if the foe chosen does not have them.

Therefore if you believe, as Labour officially does, that the close relationship with America on the world stage, where the two more or less share a single foreign policy and world view, you have to accept that the renewal of Trident is an essential protection which cannot be abandoned in the short to medium term in a turbulent and unstable world. If Labour were to keep the same US centric foreign policy but abandon Trident, it would lose any general election it fought. Fear is the most powerful political driver for which people will never vote.

The second way of looking at things, which is one which I think has merit for Labour to consider, is to conclude Britain now needs to evolve a distinctive foreign policy of its own. This would involve a detachment from America's endless need to be top dog no matter what. The Cold War is over and it is in Britain's best interests to detach itself from Western attempts to start a new one.

Instead Britain should have the courage, for the first time since the fall of its empire, to become truly independent, based on the reality of the world as it is and the economic challenge facing the former imperial power. It should seek good diplomatic relations with

Russia and China which benefit both sides. To a degree this is already happening with China, but with Russia relations are frozen into a 'blame the Russians formula' which is negative in outlook and effect. Historically Russia is one of Britain's oldest allies.

Indeed the potential threats to the world ahead come not from imperial ambitions but from militant Islam (which could acquire nuclear weapons though a takeover in Pakistan) or some fruitcake dictator who seizes power somewhere. Some kind of collapse of the communist rule in China could have very bad outcomes as well as positive ones, although the Chinese version of one party rule is very different from the failed Soviet model. In all of these scenarios Russia is an ally. When Europe is threatened, whether from the Ottomans, Napoleon, the Kaiser or Hitler, Russia has at some point played a decisive role in its defence and survival.

Meanwhile China has embraced its own unique interpretation of capitalism and become the second economic country of the world. So long as its governance evolves (rather like our gradual transition from absolute monarchy) to a format which keeps pace with public acceptance, there is no rational process which would cause China to provoke a conflict, which could risk all it has achieved. Indeed there is much that China admires about Britain and much that it feels it can learn. When the British Queen and the Chinese President sit together as Heads of State, the common factor is neither is elected. Eventually there are likely to be elections within the communist system and then in time there will be competing threads within it.

Nevertheless the idea that these two vast countries, Russia and China, are going to do things our way is silly; they have their own structures and traditions which fly in the face of much we hold dear. But as long as they do not seek to impose them on us, we would make much more progress by engagement and the promotion of mutual interests than will ever be the case by provocation, confrontation or exclusion. We need to remind ourselves just how much progress both have made since the days of Mao and Stalin.

Britain is now struggling with insufficient economic output to meet all the needs of its population across the range; housing, public services and infrastructural renewal are all near to crisis. The huge expansion of GDP required will not allow no go areas where we do not trade because their domestic standard falls short of our specification. Moreover we cannot allow ourselves to be dragged into any more idiotic wars on a heroic emotional tide, which cost lives, ruin countries and achieve nothing.

The goal must be to have good relations with each of the three super powers. We should also make clear that any further eastward move of NATO will be opposed, unless it involves a structural change to bring Russia and its dependencies in. In the Middle East we must have a much tougher approach to Israel and its preposterous settlement policies, formally recognise the Palestinian State (as parliament has voted to do) and be far more critical and a lot less cosy with the autocratic Gulf States which flout every concept of human rights on the one hand and arm and finance insurgencies on the other.

These changes of perspective are important. Although full of clever people, the Foreign Office is intellectually the weakest of the great offices of state and a good deal of midnight oil needs to be burned there to move off from a cold war culture. A good example is set by the City of London. If we ignore for the purpose of this argument that our financial sector is out of proportion to the rest of the economy, it is the case that London is now probably the top financial centre of the world. There is no market anywhere with which it is not connected.

We need make Britain the top diplomatic centre with good working relationships with all the strategic powers. To achieve this will require a mindset removed from imposing our values on the world, laudable though most of them are, which sees that conflict and confrontation no longer achieve any positive outcomes and actually cause huge suffering. In the foreign office there is an acute inability to make strategic assessments based on a full appreciation of the other side's red lines, fears, culture, motivation, insecurities and aims and to weave those into our own strategic plan. The FO sees everything as if a game of cricket. Maybe once upon a time, but no longer. Labour needs to be prepared to impose a new regime upon this floundering ministry.

There is a powerful case for changing the nature of our military posture away from power projection, which leads to fights against enemies of our own creation, like

Islamic State. Instead we should adopt a posture which does not threaten, but which makes the UK too tough a nut for any power to crack. There are four key battles in our nation's history thus far; Hastings, The Spanish Armada, Trafalgar and the Battle of Britain. We lost the first and it ended Saxon England as a nation. But we won the others and by doing so protected the integrity of our country. Each time it signalled to the enemy that he could not beat us.

So our defence must focus, because we are an island nation, on naval, air and cyber systems that not only cannot be broken, but which have an attrition impact upon the aggressor. We must develop the capacity (if we do not already have it) to hack into guidance systems of hostile missiles as well as be able to intercept and destroy any surviving incoming threats. We already have the science and the technological capacity; as history shows us, both are useless without the will.

Clearly if we review our vision of how the world is, a review of the nuclear deterrent can begin to make sense. To do that we need to separate the delivery platform from the warhead, since each performs a different function in the Trident package.

The idea of the submarine launched missile derived from the need to somehow make the weapons system immune from a pre-emptive first strike. In other words a nuclear Pearl Harbour. That ensured the absolute credibility of the weapon's power to deter, because even if the target country's military infrastructure and fighting capability had been destroyed, the aggressor would still end up a cinder by nightfall. It may not be an exaggeration to say that the deployment of these vessels and their armament by principally the US and the Soviets, but also by Britain and France, prevented the cold war becoming hot.

The basis of the security of the delivery platform was that nuclear powered submarines could cruise the world's oceans entirely undetected and be able to fire their missiles, whatever happened back home. This ides was developed in the late 1950s and became the British system by agreement between the US and UK in 1962, using the earlier Polaris rocket. If Trident is renewed, its projected lifespan will mean the notion of these submarines being undetectable will have lasted for nearly one hundred years. Is that realistic? Is it not a gamble?

Remember this technology predates the internet, smart phones and the whole technological revolution which now drives the world. Is it realistic to suppose that it will remain impossible to find and sink these submarines by missiles fired thousands of miles away? Is it not likely that its communications and guidance systems will in any case be hacked? Can you be satisfied that the science of detection will stand still? Moreover Britain is the only nuclear armed power which relies on the one delivery platform, so the survival of the nation is bet on a single supposition. There is no plan B.

Having introduced worries about the delivery platform, we now need to look at the nuclear capability and its origins and whether it is still effective for our purpose. The original British deterrent was the V Bomber force which carried massively powerful hydrogen bombs and was tasked to attack Warsaw Pact targets in Eastern Europe and European Russia, if the Soviets had used their significant numerical superiority of troops and armour to burst out of the iron curtain and drive to the Channel.

The initial aim was to destroy everything in the enemy rear, effectively cutting them off from reinforcements and supplies as well as command. The expectation was that the first wave of RAF bombers would kill eight to ten million people. This was of critical importance because the V Bombers were closer and would strike about two hours before the main waves of Strategic Air Command's B52 formations arrived to obliterate the heart of the Soviet empire.

This doomsday planning was seen at the time as quite rational, though not without risk. The Russians had their own bombers and Britain depended for its survival on none getting past its homeland fighter umbrella. Likewise the US, although the size of that country suggested that they could lose a city or two, whereas Britain, tiny and close packed, could not. There was also the issue of Nuclear Winter.

It was however not any of these fears or calculations which brought about change; it was the unexpected accuracy of Soviet missile defences which were somewhat in advance of Western capability at that point. First the bombers flew under the radar cover a few hundred feet off the ground, next they had standoff cruise missile type of bombs and finally they were abandoned in favour of submarine launched missiles carrying nuclear warheads.

By this time the prosecution to victory of nuclear war as an extension of diplomacy by force, was a notion abandoned by all but a clutch of deluded cranks, a few of whom existed in each of the confronting military structures. Instead, the doctrine of MAD (Mutually Assured Destruction) became the order of the day. This was not a means of defence, but of retaliation in the event of being attacked. It caused a vast build-up of nuclear armed missiles on both sides so that each had the power to destroy all life on earth several times over. It is undoubtedly the case that the greatest miracle in history is that nobody pressed the button. Trident is a product of that period. It is not playing with our national security to question whether such a system is in tune with the reality of our times.

The problem with Trident is that it is a strategic platform designed for destruction on a scale difficult to imagine and its deterrent value derives from the notion that Soviet Russia might, just might, have been willing to annihilate Britain as a forward base for American military operations, calculating that the US would not be willing to risk its civilisation being fried to protect its ally. The fact that this form of deterrence is substantially American (with British boats armed with British built warheads to US pattern) derives from the Kennedy Administration's extreme discomfort with the idea that its ally, who was not forgiven for Suez, had the power to independently start a nuclear war.

Two considerations spring from this arrangement. It is a clear expectation that the foreign policy of the United Kingdom will be in step with that of the US and that its deterrent is for all practical purposes subject to US political and infrastructural support. The missiles are actually leased from the US, not bought. From that the fundamental truth springs. The Trident deterrent is not really independent (like France's entirely home built warheads and missiles) and because of that neither is The UK. The hand in hand geopolitical history of the two countries post 9/11, however mistaken the policy or damaging the outcome, underscores this.

It could be argued in the Cold War that the survival of the UK was dependent on the protection of the US. Whatever the hawks in the Pentagon may say or project, this is simply no longer the case. Indeed the reverse may well be true. Such is the strategic overspend of the US today that it is actually creating new threats to itself and its allies. The question I believe should be asked by UK politicians is whether Britain should once more assert its independence in its dealings with the world at large, and if so, how any threat to that independence can be deterred.

When the question is distilled down to that basic premise, Trident falls short by a margin on four counts. First, the security from detection cannot be guaranteed for the lifetime of the upgraded new submarines. Second, the sheer destructive power of the weapon and its consequences might induce the calculation by an enemy that we would shrink from using it. Third, hacking science might advance sufficiently to bring it down on our own heads. Fourth, it puts all our deterrent eggs in one basket.

What is needed is flexible and dispersed deterrent power that strikes at the heart of the aggressor's offensive weapons platform, neutralising his ability to harm and damage. This will in part come from cutting edge capability in the secretive realm of cyber warfare and it is there that the UK should direct a priority effort both for defence and attack.

For the deterrent package to be complete the neutralising cyber power must be backed by enough force to punish. Here caution is needed. First of all it is important to remember that weapons systems look omnipotent when they are designed, but can become obsolete when deployed. The arrow, the cannon, the battleship and the bomber have all slipped from the pedestal of the ultimate weapon. Older readers will remember the enormous deterrent authority of HMS Hood, which when combat came survived for less than five minutes.

The missile may be going that way too, but for the medium term it will remain important. So will the submarine, but perhaps in a more flexible format than the Trident proposal. To be credible the deterrent needs to be usable and whilst devastating, its power should be short of a doomsday scenario which kills millions. MAD required the doomsday element. Deterring a modern aggressor will require something more sophisticated and more flexible.

There is, unless we provoke it, no nuclear threat to the UK today from either of the remaining strategic powers, Russia and China, both of whom are nuclear armed. They each see the US as threatening and they also see her as bullying. Russia maintains parity with US MAD systems and China is building towards that position. Neither country sees the UK as a threat, unless it is used as a platform to challenge them. The UK, Russia and China share increasing economic interests and none could possibly benefit from obliterating each other.

The threat, if there is one, comes from some irrational regime in a tactical nuclear power, or a state seeking to become one. To deter that threat (given that their platforms are too primitive to lend themselves to cyber neutralisation) a flexible punch is required which would avoid vast civilian homicide, but would degrade and destroy a challenging military (conventional or nuclear) capability in a single strike. It is not practical in this narrative to prescribe the form or specification of this twin deterrent project, but it is clear that we are one of the world's cyber warfare powers and with the Vanguard (there is no reason why the upgrade of these vessels should not proceed) and Astute classes of submarine, we have the industrial and naval capacity to create a flexible deterrent which is usable without ending the world, and therefore likely in the modern context to be more credible.

Whether the warheads are low yield tactical nuclear of up to 3 kilotons, or high explosive would remain both a political and military option. Critical would be the ability to penetrate hardened bunkers and deep underground installations. This approach offers Labour the ability to cast doubt on the credibility and reliability of Trident going forward. It offers instead a robust alternative *more likely* to keep Britain safe, coupled to a re-boot of foreign policy tailored to British interests, not of the past, but of the now and the tomorrow.

Above all the advice must be never to link the cost of keeping Britain safe with the social advantage of spending elsewhere. Preserving the integrity of these islands, the safety of the people, their freedom, their heritage, their culture and the fabric of their homeland is priceless, and a first requirement above all others. No party which is seen to be uncommitted to that priority will ever get itself elected and Labour in all its wings must accept that.

Had the political authorities decided to spend the money used to build the radar infrastructure that enabled our pilots to win the Battle of Britain on some other needy project, and there were many claimants in the1930s, the swastika may be flying over our public buildings even today. The fate of nations often turns on quite small hinges. That is a lesson never to forget.

Labour cannot be seen to have a lax attitude to national security, nor can it afford in the current electoral climate to give moral aspirations priority over practical demands to keep the country safe. Just to abandon the nuclear deterrent on its own will not do. What can be done is to cast doubt about the deterrent potential of a renewed Trident system and then to demonstrate that a different approach will be better secure the country from attack. Labour has to offer the more credible, and therefore the safer option.

Economic Competence

There is a fundamental problem with the UK economy. It stems from a failure to manage the transition from making things for consumption in the Empire, to makings things for consumption in competitive world markets. Following on from that came poor industrial relations turning home investment from manufacturing to services, which led to an economy based on consumption and not on wealth creation. A failure to realign the value of the currency to reflect these trends left it riding at a margin which made imports very cheap and exports very expensive. Talk of rebalancing the economy has led to nothing.

The consequence of this is that not only is the economy a good deal smaller than it should be, but it is also unable to deliver the tax revenue sufficient to pay for all the services and infrastructure that its people expect. This leads to burgeoning government debt and cuts in public services which increases the gap between rich and poor. Put simply assets are valued higher than labour.

Because New Labour had failed to heed the warnings which led to the financial crash and was then completely inept at defending itself from the charge that it alone was responsible for a worldwide disaster which actually began in the US, it has allowed the fiction to develop that it is the Tories who are big on economic wisdom. In truth the never ending litany of missed forecasts and failure to balance the books indicates the Tories haven't a clue. But they are really good at working the system so that capital prospers at the expense of the hard working people who pay both in cuts to their services and benefits and in the never ending cycle of borrowing to meet the cost of housing, childcare and other essentials of life. And guess who profits from that.

Labour now has to go on the attack to expose this so called Tory economic recovery for the sham that it is, and it must offer a complete change of direction. It is no good to go to the country with an ambition to halt austerity based on the economic practices already entrenched, which is why careful study of the process of *Dynamic Quantitative Easing* is essential, as there is no other way out of the debt fuelled gridlock. The economic cycle no longer is a traditional cycle of production, consumption, destocking and restocking. It is a debt cycle. When consumers max out they stop buying. When they pay down a bit, they buy again. The best growth you will ever get from that is to bump along at the bottom.

At the moment the UK economy delivers GDP of approximately £1.8 trillion and tax revenue of £520 billion. Right now we need an economy of £2.2 trillion and tax revenue of £800 billion to achieve all the standards we aspire to in health, education, infrastructure, work life balance and career opportunity which politicians endlessly promise and never deliver.

Labour needs to be able to demonstrate it has a plan to achieve first of all a great leap forward to where we should actually be now, and then to go on and achieve 5% growth each year for ten years. That will put Great Britain back to where it should be. Those figures are utterly beyond the scope of the debt fuelled shopping fest driven by house price inflation. The vested interests of the bloated finance industry will fight tooth and nail to retain the current economic model. Labour must demonstrate that the Tory good life is not only not as good as it could be, but enslaves people in a debt cycle which sucks money from the many to the few. Labour must then offer a radical and convincing alternative which really does offer a new economic settlement.

We have already looked at Central Banks and Quantitative Easing. To re-cap QE involves the bank buying in government debt and sometimes company debentures of good quality. New money is being created to purchase these assets in order to increase the supply of currency. As has been said before, money is a measure not a commodity, and if it is used in this way it is essentially measuring debt. This has the effect of inflating assets and increasing the supply of available debt through bank lending, too often to purchase more assets. This is the very last thing the unbalanced UK economy needs.

DQE (*Dynamic Quantitative Easing*) measures new wealth creation, not debt. It must be new money issued by the Treasury, not the Central Bank, and must flow directly into the base of the economy as cash to fund social house building, new roads, railways, power stations, schools, hospitals etc., which will increase GDP and re-energise the base of the economy without increasing debt. The economic growth resulting will increase the tax flow, especially if the taxation reforms proposed earlier are enacted. Careful matching of money flow to capacity is essential to avoid excessive inflation, but incomes will rise. So will interest rates, allowing a much better return on savings which will increase. In spite of this the value of sterling will fall to a more competitive level because there will be more of it flowing within the economy debt free.

This issue of sterling devaluation, which should be a by-product of DQE, is critical. An overvalued currency favours capital but bears down heavily on labour. Exports have to become more competitive, imports have to become more expensive, and home production of consumer needs and fancies must once again become the backbone of an industrialised economy adapted to the digital and technological age. An organised realignment of sterling by increasing its supply in a measured way to reflect an increase in economic output, is not to be confused with a collapse in value through a loss of confidence brought about by indiscriminate printing of worthless money.

Timing, skill and judgement will be required to balance the release of new money, the availability of resources and labour, the fall in the value of the pound, the increase in productivity and the move to home production of consumer goods and food, coupled with an increase in exports. Exports will become cheaper but imports, including raw materials and energy, will become more expensive. Incomes will rise, but nothing must happen either too fast or not fast enough. Decisions will need to be taken and most, if not all, of these will be political.

This is why control of the management of the economy has to be taken from the Bank of England, which is not a democratic institution nor a political ministry. The BoE must retain responsibility for the integrity of the banking system, as it did successfully for decades before fumbling reforms and deregulation led to a complete financial collapse and taxpayer rescue. Trying to guide the economy with committees of experts who sit on their hands year after year and do nothing but waffle and make flawed forecasts has been an interesting experiment whose time has run out.

What Labour must take on board is this. It will not be enough to borrow a bit more, spend a bit more, tax a bit more and generally offer a better deal. To win convincingly and make a difference, it has to revisit the principle followed by Attlee. It is not about policy. It is about the system. Young people especially sense instinctively that the system is failing. They know it is failing them and even if they are doing alright individually, they are uneasy that too much is unfair to too many.

An economic settlement which gives the top one per cent as much as the other ninety nine per cent combined, cannot sustain and is not acceptable. Almost everything which has happened since Thatcher has favoured capital at the expense of labour. Yet without labour, capital is nothing. The Labour Party must live up to its name, stop dancing on a sixpence in the political centre, rediscover its reforming zeal and show that it has a radical programme which will restore the balance. To do that the system itself has to change.

That is what this Road Map is about.

Afterword

Labour Must Be Ready

Looking forward to 2020 is not easy as I write this in 2016. There are headwinds building up in the global economy, we do not know if we will still be in the EU or should we make the mistake of voting to leave, if the United Kingdom will still be intact. So an incoming Labour government could have a daunting in tray of critical issues. For ordinary people leading ordinary lives, whatever the great historical shifts, the frustrations and opportunities tend to remain the same. Health, housing, education, income, jobs and work life balance. Labour must always be ready to look after the small things that make a big impact on everyday life.

The ideas in the Road Map, properly refined and tuned, will help Labour to win power, but that will bring responsibility for a much bigger agenda for government. This will include a multitude of issues which affect people in a direct way. They will look to the new government for action. Labour must be ready to hit the ground running and not waste a lot of time on spin and presentation without much happening, as New Labour did in 1997. Policies to ignite significant and sustained economic growth, the nuclear deterrent, re-nationalising monopoly public utilities such as railways and power generation, immigration, housing and healthcare as well as electoral reform, all have to be resolved in opposition and put into effect at the outset of government. But so must little details which affect the quality of life for the hard pressed.

A Labour victory will signal a public attitude for change. Brits generally are averse to change, but when they decide the time has come to move on they like to move fast. Labour cannot kick the can down the road with consultation processes, studies by experts and constitutional commissions, nor hide behind golden rules. Fully decided, rehearsed and costed Labour must have its plans ready and change must begin on the morning of the very first day. That is the nature of a dynamic shift in the political weather. It happens because those who inspire and lead it know where they are going. It will take judgment, passion, conviction, energy and courage. Labour must show it has all those qualities, which will energize the whole nation as we advance together to new and better times.

9781533159762